Deserts

KINGFISHER

Kingfisher Publications Plc
New Penderel House
283–288 High Holborn
London WC1V 7HZ
www.kingfisherpub.com

First published by Kingfisher Publications Plc 2005
2 4 6 8 10 9 7 5 3 1
1TR/0105/PROSP/RNB(RNB)/140MA/F

ISBN 0 7534 1100 8

Editor: Jennifer Schofield
Senior designer: Carol Ann Davis
Cover designer: Poppy Jenkins
Picture manager: Cee Weston-Baker
DTP manager: Nicky Studdart
Production controller: Jessamy Oldfield

Printed in China

Acknowledgements
The publishers would like to thank the following for permission to reproduce their material. Every care has been taken
to trace copyright holders. However, if there have been unintentional omissions or failure to trace copyright holders,
we apologise and will, if informed, endeavour to make corrections in any future edition.
b = bottom, c = centre, l = left, t = top, r = right

Cover: Alamy/Lenscapp; page 1: Getty Imagebank; 2–3 Corbis/Firefly Productions; 4–5 Corbis/Gavriel Jecan; 6–7 Getty Taxi; 8t Panoramic
Images/Warren Marr; 8b Corbis/Dean Conger; 9t Corbis/Michael & Patricia Fogden; 9b Corbis/Owen Franken; 10–11 Still Pictures/
Frans Lemmens; 11t Corbis/Peter Johnson; 11b Corbis/Peter Johnson; 12–13 Corbis/Peter Lillie; Gallo Images; 12t Panoramic Images/
Warren Marr; 12b Science Photo Library/David Scharf; 14–15 Getty Taxi; 14b Getty Imagebank; 15tr Corbis/Dewitt Jones;
15br Corbis/Martin Harvey; Gallo Images; 16–17 Getty National Geographic; 16cr Getty Imagebank; 16b NHPA/Darryl Balfour;
17cl NHPA/Martin Harvey; 17r Corbis; 18–19 Ardea/John Cancalosi; 18 Ardea/Pat Morris; 19 Minden Pictures ; 20–21 Corbis; 20cl Minden
Pictures; 20b Frank Lane Picture Agency; 21tr Michael & Patricia Fogden; 21br NHPA/Daniel Heuclin; 22–23 Getty Imagebank;
22cr Corbis/Martin Harvey; Gallo Images; 23tr Ardea/Ken Lucas; 24–25 Getty Photographer's Choice; 25tr Corbis/Hans Georg Roth;
26–27 Still Pictures; 27tr Corbis/Richard Powers; 28–29 Still Pictures; 29tr Corbis/Derek Trask; 30–31 Still Pictures; 30b Corbis/Janet Jarman;
31tr Science Photo Library/Peter Ryan; 32–33 Corbis/KM Westermann; 32bl Getty Imagebank; 33br Getty Imagebank; 34–35 Getty Stone;
34cl Corbis; 35t Corbis/Carl & Ann Purcell; 35c Corbis/Paul A Souders; 36–37 Corbis/Sergio Pitamitz; 36b Getty Stone; 37br Corbis/
Hughes Martin; 38–39 Science Photo Library/Martin Bond; 38b British Museum; 39t Getty National Geographic; 39b Corbis/James L Amos;
40–41 Alamy/Steve Bloom; 41t Getty National Geographic; 48 Corbis/ Nigel J Dennis; Gallo Images

Commissioned artwork on page 7 by Encompass Graphics
Commissioned photography on pages 42–47 by Andy Crawford. Project-maker and photoshoot co-ordinator: Miranda Kennedy
Thank you to models Lewis Manu and Rebecca Roper

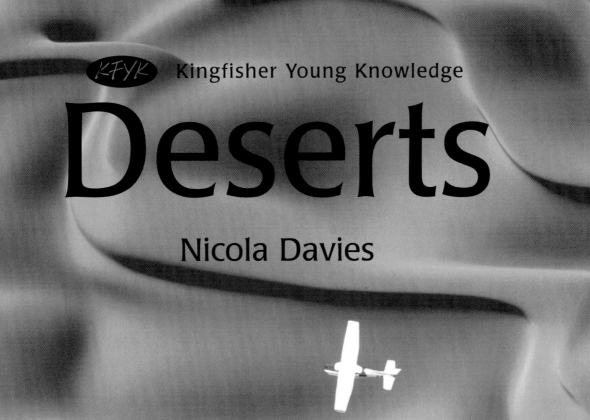

KFYK **Kingfisher Young Knowledge**

Deserts

Nicola Davies

Contents

What is a desert?

A desert is a place where it almost never rains. This makes these areas the driest places on earth and the hardest to live in.

All around the world

A quarter of our planet is covered in deserts. Wherever there is desert, there are animals and plants that have found a way to survive the harsh, dry conditions.

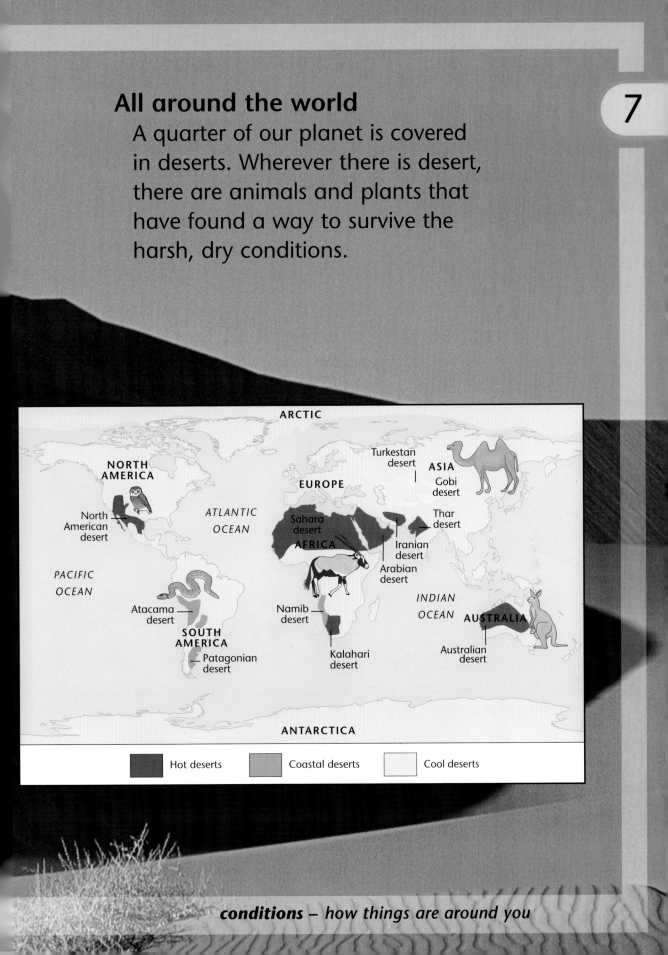

ARCTIC

NORTH AMERICA

EUROPE

ASIA

Turkestan desert

Gobi desert

North American desert

ATLANTIC OCEAN

Sahara desert

AFRICA

Thar desert

Iranian desert

Arabian desert

PACIFIC OCEAN

Atacama desert

Namib desert

INDIAN OCEAN

AUSTRALIA

SOUTH AMERICA

Patagonian desert

Kalahari desert

Australian desert

ANTARCTICA

Hot deserts   Coastal deserts   Cool deserts

conditions – how things are around you

Looking different

Not all deserts are hot and sandy. They can be pebbly, cool, rocky, mountainous or even a mixture of these. Every desert is unique!

Hot Mojave

The Mojave in North America was once the bottom of a lake. Now, it is a huge plain covered in cracked, dried mud and pebbles.

Cool Gobi

In Mongolia's Gobi desert, the wind always blows from the same direction. This shapes the sand dunes and pushes them forward.

plain – a flat surface

Hot Sahara

These rocks are found in mountains that are part of the Sahara. They are so high that, in the winter, they are covered in frost.

Coastal desert

Fog blows in from the sea next to the Namib desert. This brings water to some of the highest sand dunes in the world.

og – a low cloud of tiny drops of water

Wild weather

Desert weather is extreme. Clear blue skies mean that deserts are almost always sunny and hot during the day. But, at night, it is a very different story.

Chilly nights

With no clouds to keep in the day's warmth, nights in the desert are very cold. Desert people light fires to keep warm after dark.

extreme weather – very hot or cold

Roasting days

It may be freezing at midnight, but by midday in the desert, it is really hot. Animals, such as these springboks, have to shelter from the sun.

Keeping warm... and cool

Desert squirrels use their bushy tails to help them cope with the extremes of weather. In the cold night, the squirrel's tail is like a fluffy blanket. But, during the hot day, it is a perfect sunshade.

Whistling wind

Deserts are so windy that almost every one has a wind with its own special name. For example, the wind in Algeria is called the Khamsin, and in North America, it is called the Chubaseos.

Dusty gusts!
Sometimes, desert winds pick up sand and dust, and blow them around in storms that can last for days. This makes it hard to see and even to breathe.

gusts – sudden blasts of wind

Sandy sculpture

Gusts full of sand and dust slowly wear away
rocks. Over thousands of years, the rocks
are transformed into strange shapes, such
as these rocks found in the Mojave desert.

Smoothest sands

Desert wind rubs the
sand grains together.
This makes the grains
smooth and round.

transformed – changed

Desert rain

Rain in the desert is very rare. So, when there are showers, desert plants and animals have to make the most of them.

Stormy weather

Heavy rain often follows thunder and lightning. In some deserts, storms bring rain every year, but other deserts can stay dry for more than ten years.

rare – when something does not happen often

Be quick!

As soon as it rains, frogs lay their eggs in the rainwater pools. Their tadpoles must grow quickly and change into frogs before the pools dry out.

Beautiful blooms

Desert plants flower after the rain, so the whole desert looks like a carpet of blossoms. When the flowers dry out and die, they leave seeds behind. These seeds sprout the next time it rains.

tadpoles – *young frogs and toads*

Prickly plants

Desert plants are tough. They have thicker skins, smaller leaves and more spines than other plants. This stops the heat from drying them up, and keeps hungry mouths away.

Drop that leaf!
Creosote bushes from North America drop their leaves when it is dry. But, when it rains, they grow them again.

The Namib's dew collector
Leaves of the strange-looking welwitschia plant bend over onto the ground. Fog and dew stick to the leaves, making droplets of water that run down to the roots.

Lots of spikes

Saguaro cacti from Arizona
have no leaves. Instead,
they store water in their
huge stems. These stems
are protected by thick skin
and lots of prickly spikes.

Hide and seek!

Only the tops of the stone
plant's two fat leaves peek
above the ground's surface.
The plant hides from the
sun and drying winds until
it rains and it can flower.

Dew – small drops of water that form in the night on grass and plants

Desert fliers

Flight makes desert life easier for birds because they can travel long distances to find food and water. But they still have to cope with the hot days and cold nights.

Burrow nester

The tiny elf owl makes use of the cool twilight to hunt for small mammals, reptiles and insects. It nests underground where its eggs are protected from the fierce heat that could easily cook them in their shells.

twilight – when it is not dark or light, at dawn and at dusk

Cacti surgeons

Woodpeckers make holes in the rotten or broken stems of giant saguaro cacti. The woodpeckers nest in the cool holes and peck away any sick parts of the cactus. This stops disease from spreading to the whole plant.

Roadrunner stretches

Desert roadrunners warm up after the cold desert night by lifting their neck feathers and letting the sun shine on a patch of special skin. This skin soaks up heat and keeps them warm.

Little creatures

Insects, reptiles and rodents thrive in the desert because they do not need much water. They can also hide from the heat, wind or cold in burrows.

Honey tummies

Desert honey ants store precious water and nectar in their blown-up tummies. This store helps the ant colony to survive when there is no food or water.

Sleep by night

Reptiles like this chuckwalla stay underground in the cold of the night. When morning comes, they lie in the sun to warm up.

burrows – holes or tunnels under the ground

Fog bathers
Darkling beetles find something to drink by tapping the droplets of water from fog on their legs, and tipping them towards their mouths.

Sleep by day
Animals like this little gerbil are warm-blooded. They search for food in the cold night, but in the day they need to hide underground in burrows to keep cool.

warm-blooded – body temperature that is always warm

Mighty mammals

Large mammals that live in deserts cannot shelter from the sun in burrows like their smaller relatives. So, they must find other ways to beat the heat

Dig out to chill out

To cool their tummies, kangaroos scrape away at the hot surface sand and lie down on the colder sand underneath.

mammals – warm-blooded animals that feed their young on mother's milk

Colour-coded

Fennec foxes' pale fur helps to reflect the heat and keep them cool – just like a white T-shirt will keep you cool on a hot summer's day.

Camel cooler

At night, camels' bodies become really cold. So, although the sun warms them all day, they are never too hot.

reflect – send back or aside

Pools of water

Rivers flowing through the desert or bubbling up from under the ground can bring water all year round to deserts. A place where this happens is called an oasis.

Green and growing

Oases are bustling with life. Tall trees, such as palms, and many kinds of animals can live in oases because there is plenty of water.

bustling – *busy*

Walking to water

Oases are very important to desert people and their animals. They may travel hundreds of kilometres to find water at a familiar oasis – even if the water is at the bottom of a well.

well – a deep hole in the ground with water at the bottom

Desert dwellers

People have lived in deserts for thousands of years. They have learned all sorts of ways to cope with the difficulties of desert life.

People who wander

Many desert people are nomads. They live in tents and move about to find fresh water and grazing for their animals.

nomads – people who move from place to place, taking their homes with them

Water carriers
Women in India's
Thar desert carry
water from far-away
wells in large jars
that they balance
on their heads.

Growing deserts

Deserts are important and beautiful wild places. But, they are expanding unnaturally because of some of the things that humans do. Every year, desert swallows up valuable grassland, farmland and forest.

Too much munching

Where people let their animals eat all the plants, the sun and wind can hit the bare ground. This turns the soil into dust and makes it difficult to regrow plants.

expanding – *getting bigger*

Bad gas!

Cars, aeroplanes and industry emit gases that make the weather hotter. This is called global warming. It is worse in places that are already hot and dry, so it makes deserts grow.

emit – give off

Making deserts green

People can help to stop deserts from expanding by planting trees and grass to protect the soil. Irrigating the desert helps to keep the plants alive.

Rain saving

Saving rainwater with dams mean that there will be water for crops. This woman is harvesting food in what was once desert.

irrigating – *watering big areas, such as whole fields*

Magic water

Usually water runs through sand and is lost. Adding flakes of special plastic to the water helps soil to hold on to it and the plants to grow.

Green... and greener

Growing plants also helps to cool the ground and the air above. This means that the soil stays moist and the desert cannot expand.

moist – damp

Cities in the desert

There are cities in deserts all over the world. But, cities with millions of people use a lot of water – and that is a big problem in any desert!

Bright lights, big city

Las Vegas, in America's Nevada desert, is so big that it uses water from hundreds of miles away. This lack of water threatens both the wildlife and farmland with drought.

drought – a long period of time when there is no water

Green, green city

Abu Dhabi, on the coast of the United Arab Emirates, uses fresh water from the sea by taking out the salt! This means there is enough water to create green spaces that keep the city cool.

Ways to save water

Kerzaz, an ancient city in the Sahara, needs far less water than a modern town. People there use water carefully and know that every drop is very precious.

Using the desert

Deserts may look empty, but they have hidden treasures. They also give us the space to do things that are dangerous anywhere else.

Deadly testing

The world's deadliest weapons, nuclear bombs, are tested in deserts where they cannot kill anyone. But, these bombs leave the land poisoned for many years after testing.

Hidden energy

Petroleum oil is found under some deserts. It is pumped and carried to cities and other countries in huge pipes like this one.

Underground jewels

Opals were formed
millions of years ago
when water drained
from rocks under
the ground. This
ground is now the
Australian desert
and almost all of
the world's opals
are mined there!

etroleum oil – *the oil used to make fuel for cars, electricity and many plastics*

Lots of fun!

Sunny blue skies and beautiful scenery make deserts great places to relax, but some people prefer a bit more action.

Sandboarding

You can go down a sand dune in just the same way that you would slide down a snowy slope. You can even surf a dune like a big wave in the sea!

Desert racer

Sandbuggies can climb steep dunes and zoom about the desert without getting stuck in the sand. They are great fun but their tyres can damage desert plants.

Comfortable climbing

Rock formations found in deserts are warm and dry. This makes them easier to climb than mountains where the weather can be cold, wet and icy.

History in the desert

We can learn about the past in deserts because the hot, dry air preserves dead bodies. Sand covers the dried remains of people, plants and animals and, because few people live in the deserts, they can lie undisturbed for a long time.

Mummies from long ago

Bodies buried in deserts dry out very quickly, so skin, hair and clothes can last for thousands of years. Preserved dead bodies, called mummies, found in deserts show us how people looked and dressed a long time ago.

Rock art

Thousands
of years ago,
people painted
pictures on rocks in the
Namib. They show that the desert
used to be grassland bustling
with people and animals.

Desert dinos

Some of the world's most
exciting dinosaur fossils
have been found in deserts.
The dry winds wear away
the rock, and bring fossil
bones close to the surface.

ossils – the remains of ancient animals or plants turned to rock

Ice and water

Not all deserts are hot and dusty – some are not even dry! The word desert can also be used to describe places where conditions are simply too tough for life to survive.

Lifeless blue

There can be no life in the sea without phyto-plankton. In places where plankton does not grow, the sea can be a wet and salty desert.

cy deserts

Some parts of the Arctic receive less rain than Africa's Sahara desert. These areas are too cold and dry for anything to grow. Polar bears survive by walking to the sea to catch seals.

phyto-plankton – the tiny floating plants found in oceans and seas

Crazy camels

Salt train

Selling salt is a very important way for desert people to make money. Loads of salt are carried across the desert on camels.

camel template

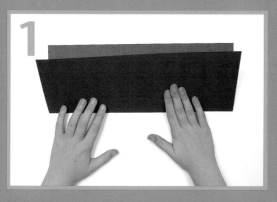

You will need
- Brown card
- Tracing paper
- Pencil
- Scissors
- Permanent marker
- Foil chocolate wrappers
- Glue
- Gold or silver thread

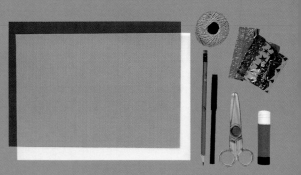

1

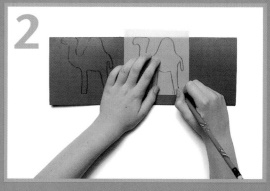

Fold the brown card in half. Put the piece of tracing paper over the camel template and trace over the camel shape.

2

Put the traced template onto the card so that the camel's hump is on the fold. Trace the camel onto the card to make three camels.

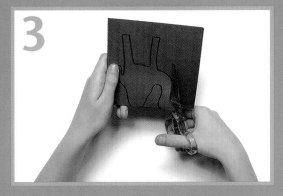

Using the scissors, carefully cut out the three camel shapes. Make sure that you do not cut through the humps at the fold.

Holding the camel firmly with one hand, use the permanent marker to draw the eyes and mouth on each camel.

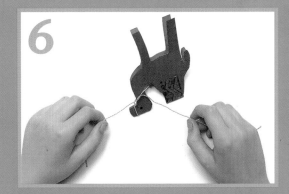

Smooth out three different foil chocolate wrappers. Paste them over the middle of the camels' backs. You may need to cut the wrappers if they are too long.

To make the camels' bridles, tie thread around the camels' necks. Use the thread to join the camels together so that they are ready to carry salt across the desert.

3-D cactus

Slit and slide!

The saguaro cactus can be over 10 metres tall and can have five arms. Some saguaro are over 200 years old!

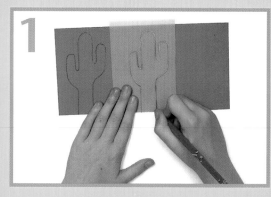

Trace the cactus template onto the tracing paper. Then, use the template to trace two cacti onto the green card.

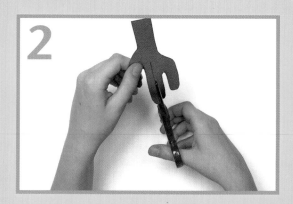

Cut out the two cactus shapes. Following the template, use the scissors to cut a slit half-way down one cactus.

slit 1
(step 2)

cactus
template

slit 2
(step 3)

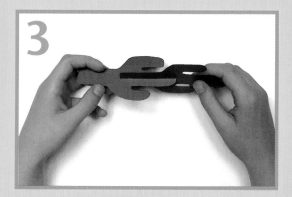

Cut a slit half-way up the second cactus. Slide the first cactus into the second. If you like, decorate the cactus with green glitter.

Palm trees

Bend and shape it!

Palm trees are often found at oases in the Sahara. Desert people rest in the shade of the palms when it is hot.

You will need
- 2 strips of brown card
- glue
- Green card
- Double-sided tape
- Shoebox lid
- Sand

1

To make the palm's trunk, glue the brown card to make an 'L' shape. Fold the card over itself to make a concertinaed tube.

2

To make the palm's leaves, cut the green card into five curved strips. Fold each strip like a fan and it will spring open.

Fill a shoebox lid with sand and put the camels, 3-D cactus and palm tree in the tray to create your own desert landscape.

3

Cut a small piece of double-sided tape and stick it in the middle of the palm's trunk. Stick each of the five leaves onto the trunk.

Aboriginal spinning top

Clever symbols

The Aboriginal people of Australia's desert painted symbols on rocks. Now, artists use these symbols to paint modern art.

You will need
- Pencil
- Mug
- Cup
- Side plate
- Card
- Scissors
- Paint
- Paintbrush
- Moulding dough
- Compass
- Chopstick

emu

campfire

child

1

To make five disks, draw on the card around a mug two times, a cup two times and a side plate once. Carefully cut out each disk.

2

Paint the disks using orange or yellow paint – if you like, each circle can be a different colour. Leave the disks to dry thoroughly.

Following the examples on page 46, paint one side of each disk with a different Aboriginal symbol. When the paint is dry, turn the disks over and paint the same symbol on the other side.

Put a ball of moulding dough under the middle of each disk. Use the point of the compass to pierce a hole in the middle of each disk.

When all five disks are on the chopstick, stand the top upright and spin it around.

To put the disks on the chopstick, start with one of the disks from the cup and the mug, then the disk from the plate and the last two from the mug and cup. The disks should be evenly spaced.

Index